ICNC **SPECIAL REPORT** SERIES

From the Hills to the Streets to the Table

Civil Resistance and Peacebuilding in Nepal

Subindra Bogati and Ches Thurber

Table of Contents

Summary 1

Introduction 3

An Integrated Framework of Civil Resistance and Peacebuilding 7

Background to Conflict in Nepal 10

STAGE 1: **Latent Conflict, 1991–1996** 12
    Features of the Conflict Phase 12
    Peacebuilding Strategies 13
    Civil Resistance Strategies 13
    Impact 14

STAGE 2: **Overt Conflict, 1996–2006** 16
    Features of the Conflict Phase 16
    Peacebuilding Strategies 19
    Civil Resistance Strategies 20
    Impact 23

STAGE 3: **Conflict Settlement, 2006–2008** 25
    Features of the Conflict Phase 25
    Peacebuilding Strategies 26
    Civil Resistance Strategies 28
    Impact 30

STAGE 4: **Post-Settlement, 2008–Present** 31
    Features of the Conflict Phase 31
    Peacebuilding Strategies 33
    Civil Resistance Strategies 35
    Impact 37

Key Takeaways 39

Cited Bibliography 42

About the Authors 44

Tables

TABLE 1: **Dynamics of civil resistance and peacebuilding across four stages of conflict in Nepal** 6

TABLE 2: **Civil resistance and peacebuilding strategies and impacts during the four stages of conflict transformation** 9

SUMMARY

THIS CASE STUDY BUILDS ON Véronique Dudouet's 2017 ICNC Special Report, *Powering to Peace: Integrated Civil Resistance and Peacebuilding Strategies*. Utilizing Dudouet's framework, we trace the development of conflict in Nepal over the past thirty years, with a specific emphasis on the 2006 civil resistance campaign and subsequent peace process that led to the resolution of the country's decade-long Maoist insurgency.

From 1996 until 2006, Nepal experienced a civil war that resulted in over 16,000 casualties. Remarkably, the conflict ended when Maoist insurgents forged an agreement with the country's political parties to jointly launch a civil resistance campaign to oust the king. This civil resistance campaign succeeded in overthrowing the king. The former rebels have since been integrated into normal democratic politics—even holding the premiership on multiple occasions—and Nepal has not seen a reversion to large-scale violence. However, many of the social tensions that initiated the conflict still have not been resolved. Nepal continues to be afflicted by armed violence and insecurity and is struggling to re-establish political stability.

What were the drivers of social and political conflict in Nepal that led to the 2006 civil resistance campaign? How were the Maoists convinced to transition from armed insurgency to civil resistance? What accounts for the success and failures of the subsequent peace process? Leveraging the Dudouet framework, we trace the trajectory of conflict from a period of latent conflict with high levels of horizontal inequalities and structural violence to an outbreak of overt, but initially violent conflict. We then illustrate how a transition from civil war to civil resistance was made possible and led to a successful conflict settlement. However, flaws in the conflict settlement and post-conflict phases have produced a turbulent post-settlement process, one that falls short of the goals of reconciliation, transitional justice, and sustainable peace.

Introduction

While civil resistance and peacebuilding have largely existed as two separate approaches to conflict transformation, new efforts are being made in scholar and practitioner communities to identify and explore linkages between the two. Véronique Dudouet's 2017 ICNC Special Report, "Powering to Peace: Integrated Civil Resistance and Peacebuilding Strategies," represents a landmark in this effort by illustrating the different assumptions and normative perspectives that underpin each approach. Building off earlier scholarship by Adam Curle, Dudouet develops a multi-stage framework for analysing the interplay of these approaches in conflict, and suggests strategies for their simultaneous implementation in the pursuit of conflict transformation.

This follow-up case study applies the framework developed by Dudouet to the conflict dynamics of Nepal over the past two and half decades. It hopes to both leverage Dudouet's framework to help better understand and explain the successes and failures of conflict transformation in Nepal, as well as to critically evaluate the strengths and limitations of the analytical framework as applied to Nepal's experiences.

Nepal represents an especially interesting case for the analysis of civil resistance and peacebuilding. It is an example of a highly unequal society where power differences between ethnic, caste, class, and religious groups create political grievances as well as an uneven playing field for social dialogue. As such, it is exactly the kind of case where we might expect peacebuilding efforts to fall short as deeply-rooted structural hierarchies of power give privileged actors little incentive to compromise. It is in this context that Dudouet suggests civil resistance could play an important role as a pre-negotiation strategy, allowing oppressed groups to use nonviolent tactics to pressure incumbents to redistribute power.

But instead of a civil resistance campaign in pursuit of the rights of oppressed groups, Nepal experienced a decade-long civil war from 1996-2006 in which over 16,000 Nepalis were killed. Remarkably, the civil war ended with an integration of civil resistance and traditional peacebuilding. The Maoist insurgents joined a coalition with other political parties to launch a nonviolent civil resistance campaign in 2006 that succeeded in forcing the king to re-establish parliament. The campaign also kick-started peace negotiations that concluded in the Comprehensive Peace Agreement (CPA) that was signed later that same year.

Thirteen years later, Nepal is a relatively peaceful, democratic country. It has avoided a return to major armed conflict, held three competitive nation-wide elections, transitioned through multiple changes of political leadership with relatively minimal violence, and finally passed a new constitution in 2015. By these measures, it is an exceptional case, avoiding the fate of so many other post-conflict environments that have been characterized by reversions to violence or authoritarian rule.

Yet Nepalis themselves are not so sanguine in their assessment of political developments over the past decade. Political gridlock during the post-settlement period prevented passage of a constitution for nearly a decade while governments have rarely lasted for more than a year.[1] Protests, strikes, and other forms of political agitation have inflicted costs on participants, bystanders, and the broader society: frequent *bandhs* (regional or nationwide general strikes) have forced citizens to forego needed income, and precipitated an increase in violent activities that occur alongside the *bandhs*. Furthermore, while there has not been a return to large-scale political violence, there has been a proliferation of armed groups in Nepal's southern plains, western hills and eastern hills.[2] Many historically marginalized communities see the political system as having failed to meet their expectations for change following the civil war, while privileged groups see the social fabric of the nation as imperiled by a reversion to sub-national identities.

This report walks through the recent history of conflict and peacebuilding in Nepal, sequentially describing each of the conflict stages in the country along the four dimensions developed in Dudouet's report.[3]

Overall, we find that Dudouet's framework provides a valuable method for understanding conflict in Nepal and that several insights from her report suggest both explanations for the successes of conflict transformation in Nepal, as well as ways that the process could have been improved. Specifically, we suggest that:

- A greater attention to peacebuilding and social inclusion in the early years of the 1990s (the "latent conflict" stage) might have helped prevent marginalized communities from seeing violence as the only way out from physical and structural oppression.

---

[1] The current prime minister, KP Sharma Oli, is the 26th prime minister since 1990.

[2] In 2009, the government claimed that 109 armed groups were active in Nepal but by 2013 armed groups' activities had essentially ceased. The high-level political talks team set up by the government in 2018 held talks with 22 different armed groups and disgruntled parties. These talks did not include a Maoist splinter group led by Netra Bikram Chand which has initiated violent activities.

[3] Dudouet's report, in turn, builds upon Adam Curle's stage-based framework for understanding conflict trajectories in contexts of power asymmetries. See: Adam Curle, *Making Peace* (London: Tavistock, 1971).

- Civil resistance, once employed by a coalition of actors, including civil society and the Maoists, succeeded in transitioning the form of overt conflict from primarily violent to primarily nonviolent.

- The civil resistance campaign also succeeded in creating political change by restoring democratic processes and pushing issues of political, economic, and social exclusion to the center of political debate.

- Greater attention to issues of social inclusion in the conflict settlement phase may have been able to prevent some of the turbulence of the post-conflict years.

We also highlight ways in which the case of Nepal requires us to build on or complicate Dudouet's framework:

- Increased awareness and mobilization around issues of structural violence can heighten the risk of physical violence when not complemented with violence prevention.

- Legacies of violent conflict can complicate the settlement and post-settlement stages of conflict as the increased "baggage" of war creates greater obstacles to security reform, social reconciliation, and transitional justice.

- Civil resistance tactics, while intended to be nonviolent, do come at a cost to participants, bystanders, and the broader society. Tactics such as general strikes can force citizens to go without income and create hardship by disrupting the larger economy. If nonviolent discipline is not maintained, mobilization can also lead to violence, deepening existing political, social and ethnic cleavages. Because of these potential costs, the use of civil resistance tactics, perhaps most especially in the post-conflict phase (by which point the society can be exhausted and have high expectations for the ongoing political transition to deliver on promises of peace and positive change), can backfire by fueling resentment from the broader society against civil resistance practitioners.

- International support can be a double-edged sword. At some points, it can be highly effective, such as when India provided a platform for dialogue that led to the Maoists transitioning to join the civil resistance campaign. But at other times it can backfire, such as when protests by disadvantaged social groups were portrayed as the subversive instruments of foreign powers, undermining their message.

The Dudouet framework offers a powerful approach for understanding conflict dynamics in Nepal, even in the rather extreme case in which overt conflict initially took the form of civil war. It also helps to highlight reasons for why the post-conflict period has fallen short of many Nepalis' expectations. As such, both the framework as well as the particular case of Nepal offer valuable lessons both for future progress in Nepal as well as for conflict transformation in other contexts.

Table 1 below presents an overview of the conflict case and identifies civil resistance and peacebuilding strategies deployed in Nepal as well as their impact along the four dimensions of conflict (from the latent to post-settlement conflict) as presented in Dudouet's report (reproduced in Table 2 on page 9).

TABLE 1: Dynamics of civil resistance and peacebuilding across four stages of conflict in Nepal.

	LATENT CONFLICT (1991–1996)	OVERT CONFLICT (1996–2006)	CONFLICT SETTLEMENT (2006–2008)	POST-SETTLEMENT (2008–PRESENT)
Features of Conflict Phase	High levels of structural inequalities; political, social and economic exclusion on the basis of ethnicity, religion, region and caste	Ten years of violent insurgency that kills 16,000 followed by 19 days of civil resistance that lead to peace negotiations	Several months of negotiations between Maoists and political parties leading to Comprehensive Peace Agreement	Continued instability as actors unable to agree on a constitutional framework or transitional justice; frequent protests and occasional violence
Civil Resistance Strategies	Increase in community organizing and civil society; marginalized groups met with repression in country's periphery	Frequent use of protest tactics by both Maoists and political parties in early 2000s culminates in joint "Jana Andolan II": a 19-day campaign of mass protest and general strike	Major protests by Madhesi groups in 2007 and 2008; use of general strikes by Maoists in 2007 to gain concessions on declaration of republic and rules for upcoming elections	All actors frequently turn to protest and strike tactics as a way of trying to gain leverage in political negotiation; creates backlash against marginalized groups
Peacebuilding Strategies	Little dialogue or violence prevention as political parties remain busy vying for power and do not believe marginalized groups present a political challenge	Attempts at negotiation between Maoists and government in early 2000s fail; dialogue between Maoists and political parties in 2005-2006 leads to coordinated civil resistance strategy and ultimately a peace agreement	Dialogue focused primarily on political next steps, rather than durable solution to underlying conflict issues	Continued efforts at dialogue, both in parliament and communities supported by substantial international assistance
Impact	Spreading awareness of injustice (heightened expectations) fuels sense of grievance and demand for change	King agrees to restore parliamentary democracy; political parties agree to negotiate with Maoists for permanent settlement	Successful completion of peace agreement, but many of the most contentious issues deferred	Nepal has experienced no return to civil war, but continued political instability

An Integrated Framework of Civil Resistance and Peacebuilding

Before delving into the Nepali case study, this section provides a brief overview of the integrated framework for civil resistance and peacebuilding developed in Dudouet's 2017 ICNC Special Report (see Table 2). Civil resistance and peacebuilding are approaches to conflict transformation that share a commitment to the pursuit of social justice through nonviolent means. They share the goal of reducing or eliminating forms of structural violence and reject the use of physical violence as a means for achieving that end.

Yet the two strategies draw from very different philosophical and practical traditions. They differ in their normative assumptions, their diagnoses of the causes of conflict, and their suggested methods for achieving social change. Peacebuilding advocates an impartial or even "pro-stability" orientation toward conflict parties, prescribes an array of methods that attempt to mitigate tension and adversity, and promotes a "multi-track" approach in which international actors often play a leading role in bringing together and promoting dialogue among local stakeholders. By contrast, civil resistance advocates a pro-justice stance, often biased in favor of challengers over incumbents and viewing instability as necessary. As such it promotes methods of contentious, extra-institutional, and even extra-legal action in an effort to put coercive pressure on incumbents and consequently shift the balance of power among actors.[4] It emphasizes a bottom-up approach, where activism emerges at the local level and national and international actors may play roles as allies or partners.

Dudouet proposes that peacebuilding and civil resistance strategies need not be alternatives, but can be employed in a complementary fashion, especially in contexts of acute power asymmetries. Building upon Curle's (1971) four-stage framework for the evolution of conflict, Dudouet identifies how civil resistance and peacebuilding strategies can be used in tandem at each stage.[5]

In Stage 1, the period of latent conflict, civil resistance tactics such as protests, strikes, and boycotts can raise awareness about inequalities and foster organization-building that paves the way for future mobilization. Meanwhile peacebuilding strategies such as preventive diplomacy and dialogue can reduce the risk of violent escalation.

---

[4] Gandhi argued that his method of *satyagraha* should rely not on coercion but rather on persuasion. Yet Gandhi's methods in practice were highly coercive and most analysts and proponents of civil resistance since have emphasized coercion as an essential part of the strategy.

[5] In addition to Curle, Dudouet's framework is also heavily informed by the work of Johan Galtung (1969, 1996), John Paul Lederach (1995, 1997), and Diana Francis (2002, 2010).

In Stage 2, the period of overt conflict, civil resistance becomes the main form of response as oppressed groups use nonviolent action to confront the state. As tensions heighten, civil resistance offers a way of empowering these groups without turning to violence.

Civil resistance may continue to be used to create pressure at the negotiating table, ensuring that negotiated outcomes do not simply reinforce existing structural hierarchies.

By Stage 3, conflict settlement, power relations have shifted toward greater balance, allowing peacebuilding tools, such as dialogue, mediation, and negotiation, to be employed in a way that can achieve social justice. Civil resistance may continue to be used to create pressure at the negotiating table, ensuring that negotiated outcomes do not simply reinforce existing structural hierarchies.

Finally in Stage 4, the post-settlement phase, peacebuilding tools such as political, security, and economic reforms, as well as reconciliation and transitional justice measures can be implemented to further advance justice and equality and address the original drivers of conflict. Again, civil resistance strategies may be used to pressure actors to make good on commitments made in the conflict settlement process.

The normative goal is not simply to end or avoid outbreaks of physical violence, but to provide a means of conflict transformation through which marginalized groups are able to address issues of structural inequality and exclusion through nonviolent, though almost certainly contentious, means. Dudouet terms this approach to conflict transformation as "constructive conflict."

Table 2 reproduces an overview of the framework from Dudouet's Special Report. The complementary approach toward conflict transformation addresses shortcomings that exist when either civil resistance or peacebuilding is used alone. Civil resistance strategies offer means of equalizing power relations and enforcing adherence to negotiated settlements that peacebuilding lacks. Meanwhile, peacebuilding methods provide tools for mitigating escalation, achieving negotiated settlements, and securing post-conflict justice that are missing from the civil resistance toolkit.

While conflicts in the real world are unlikely to proceed in so neat or linear a fashion, the framework provides an idealized model for how civil resistance and peacebuilding strategies can be used in tandem to produce a form of "constructive conflict" that has the potential to move societies from deep structural inequality toward social justice.

TABLE 2: Civil resistance and peacebuilding strategies and impacts during the four stages of conflict transformation.

	LATENT CONFLICT	OVERT CONFLICT	CONFLICT SETTLEMENT	POST-SETTLEMENT
Features of Conflict Phase	Structural violence Low awareness of conflict Power imbalance	Conflict intensification	Conflict and resistance substituted by dialogue of equals	Peace implementation and consolidation
Civil Resistance Strategies	Community organizing/mobilization Violence prevention	Nonviolent action (protest and persuasion, non-cooperation, disruptive and constructive resistance)	Popular pressure at the negotiation table for equitable bargaining outcomes	Nonviolent campaigns for full implementation of just peace
Peacebuilding Strategies	Violence prevention (early warning, preventative diplomacy, dialogue)	Peacekeeping dialogue facilitation (inter- and intra-party), human rights monitoring	Inter-party conciliation through (direct or mediated) dialogue and negotiation	Institutionalization of negotiation outcomes through political/security/socio-economic reforms, reconciliation and transitional justice
Impact	Underdog's awakening to the need for conflict to address grievances and change the status quo	Violence mitigation, empowerment of the underdog	Negotiated agreement	Sustainable peace with justice

Source: Dudouet, Véronique. *Powering to Peace: Integrated Civil Resistance and Peacebuilding Strategies.* Washington, DC: International Center on Nonviolent Conflict, 2017.

Background to Conflict in Nepal

Nepal is a country of nearly 30 million people that extends from the Indo-Gangetic Plain of South Asia to the Tibetan Plateau. Sandwiched between two major regional powers, India and China, Nepalis often refer to their country's geopolitical predicament as that of being "the yam between two boulders."

Since its unification in the middle of the 19th century, Nepal's rulers have tried to develop the country as a homogenous, monolithic and unitary state despite the highly diversified and pluralistic character of Nepali society. In so doing, these rulers conferred protection and privilege to those inhabitants whose mother tongue is the Nepali language, who are members of the upper castes (Bahuns and Chhetris) from hill regions, and who practice the Hindu faith. The legacy of this form of exclusive governance includes the unequal distribution of socio-economic resources and a political structure that reflects sharp inequalities among ethnic, linguistic and caste groups.

At the beginning of the 1990s, Nepali society was characterized by high levels of horizontal inequality and structural violence. Nepali-speaking Hindus from the highest caste groups and the middle hill region enjoyed outsized economic wealth and held the vast majority of governmental posts. Generally, indigenous nationalities,[6] Dalits (the lowest caste designation), and Madhesis (those living in the low plains region abutting India) encountered higher rates of poverty and far less access to political power.

From 1961 through 1990, Nepal was ruled through the authoritarian *panchayat* system, under which elections were held for local, regional and national councils, but political parties were banned, criticism of the king was prohibited, and civil society was stifled.

Following a wave of nonviolent revolutions around the world in the late 1980s, underground political organizations in Nepal formed a united front in 1990 and launched a civil resistance campaign, known as the *Jana Andolan* (People's Movement) demanding the implementation of multi-party parliamentary democracy. After two months of protests, the king was forced to concede to the opposition's demands. It is interesting to note that the 1990 movement was confined largely to the Kathmandu valley, which consists of three cities including the capital.

The democratic transition of 1990 allowed for greater political openness and competition. However, it fell short of meeting the hopes of all who took to the streets to demand change.

---

6   The term "indigenous" is highly contested given the ambiguous history of ancestral migration and the legal rights afforded to indigenous groups under international law. In Nepal it is generally used to refer to groups whose primary language is not Nepali and who resided in Nepal prior to the arrival of Indo-Nepali migrants from the south several hundred years ago.

In particular, no reforms were made to the country's land tenure system and the nobility retained control of the extensive land holdings they had acquired over decades of the *panchayat* system. The same ethnic and caste groups that had dominated Nepal under the monarchy continued to do so in the new democracy. While Nepal had in theory undergone a dramatic political transformation, according to some, "all that had changed were the names on the ministers' doors."[7] These enduring grievances over inequalities between social groups along ethnic, religious, caste, and geographic lines have fueled conflict in Nepal since the 1990 democratic transition.

---

7 Louise T. Brown, *The Challenge to Democracy in Nepal: A Political History* (London: Routledge, 1996), 177.

STAGE 1: Latent Conflict, 1991–1996

Features of the Conflict Phase

We begin our analysis in 1991, a year after the *Jana Andolan* civil resistance campaign. At this point in time, Nepal had passed a new constitution, held elections to a national parliament, and had formed a multiparty system of government. The monarchy still existed and the constitution ascribed the king with delimited political powers. But while the new political system introduced basic political rights and systems of elected governance, the early 1990s in Nepal still provide a classic example of a period of latent conflict. Patterns of ethnic, religious, caste-based, and geographic discrimination fueled popular grievances against dominant groups and the state.

For example, in 1996, the most privileged groups accounted for 37 percent of the population but had human development indicators 50 percent higher than other groups[8] and held 80 percent of high-level positions in parliament, the bureaucracy, and the judiciary.[9] Nepali society was also highly patriarchal, with little female involvement in political life.

While these structural inequalities had been a long-standing part of Nepali political and cultural life, prior to the democratic transition of 1990, the closed environment of the *panchayat* political system had stifled public debate about caste and ethnic relations. The regime argued that such discussions would disturb a continuing tradition of communal harmony in Nepal.[10] The mainstream Nepali intellectual and political thinking during this phase was directed towards manufacturing a narrative of ethnic harmony and a composite Nepali culture through a coercive process of "Nepalisation."

However, the book, *Fatalism and Development*, published in 1991 by Nepali scholar Dor Bahadur Bista, played a vital role in placing intergroup inequalities at the center of political discourse. The book strongly criticized the ideology of caste-based supremacy and argued that it created an obstacle to modernization and development in Nepal.[11]

Furthermore, the new political rights as enshrined in the 1990 constitution opened up space for organized collective action. Issues relating to ethnic identity, gender, caste-based

---

8   S. M. Murshed and Scott Gates, "Spatial–Horizontal Inequality and the Maoist Insurgency in Nepal," *Review of Development Economics* 9, no. 1 (2005): 121–34.

9   Paul Routledge, "Nineteen Days in April: Urban Protest and Democracy in Nepal," *Urban Studies* 47, no. 6 (May 1, 2010): 1283.

10   Krishna Bhattachan, "Ethnopolitics and ethnodevelopment: an emerging paradigm in Nepal—with a postscript," in *Nationalism and Ethnic Conflict in Nepal: Identities and Mobilisation after 1990*, eds., Mahendra Lawoti and Susan Hangen, (New York: Routledge, 2013), 35–57.

11   Dor Bahadur Bista, *Fatalism and Development: Nepal's Struggle for Modernisation* (New Delhi: Sangam Books, 1991).

discrimination and human rights came to the forefront. Different social groups, like Dalits, women, Madhesi, and indigenous nationalities, shared common experiences and narratives of marginalization, and their distinctive relationships with the state have translated into unique trajectories of resistance. As these traditionally disadvantaged groups became more aware, informed and active citizens, they led social justice campaigns to address their marginalization. Similarly, cultural associations and NGOs mushroomed and ethnic and regional political parties were established. These ethnic and regional parties raised issues of identity and exclusion that the mainstream political parties did not.

Peacebuilding Strategies

Few efforts at peacebuilding were made during this period. While some scholars, activists, and movements were beginning to raise issues of structural discrimination, political elites were focused on inter-party political competition. Furthermore, the major parties chose not to try to develop broad-based popular support through the development of platforms and programs that addressed these grievances. Instead, they embraced a top-down view of electoral politics and sought to curry favor with powerful local actors in the belief that those leaders would generate turnout at the polls. The result was little effort to seriously address issues of inequality and discrimination and a widespread disenchantment with democratic politics.

Civil Resistance Strategies

The years after 1990 saw numerous protests and strikes in Nepal, sparked by both the example of the successful *Jana Andolan* and the more open and permissive democratic environment. The strikes, commonly known as *bandhs,* came in a variety of forms and involved the shutdown of markets, colleges and schools, and transportation. The goal of the *bandhs* was to make the grievances of marginalized communities heard by a government made up mostly of members of privileged groups.

However, instead of working to consolidate democratic norms and address the genuine grievances of marginalized communities, political parties focused on toppling successive governments. They viewed the creation of intra-elite coalitions in parliament as the primary path to political power. Rather than focus on developing grassroots support, they turned their energies to trying to undermine their rivals' parliamentary coalitions. As a result, the country experienced a series of short-lived governments that provided little stability and failed to advance the people's aspirations for inclusion, economic development and good governance. The inequalities across different sectors and regions and the neglect of the periphery contributed to the dissatisfaction among rural people, especially the youth.

Impact

These new movements by marginalized groups helped raise issues related to social and economic inequality, linguistic rights, secularism, discrimination, and the recognition of diversity and identity.[12] However, the reach of these social movements was largely limited to major cities, especially Kathmandu. Many of the people engaged in these movements belonged to the middle class or elite sections of these various identity groups.

This left a window of opportunity available for another political group—the Maoists—to take advantage of dissatisfaction rooted in inter-group inequalities in Nepal's countryside. No political party or movement has mobilised the people from particular regions, ethnic and caste groups more than the Maoists.

The history of ideological Maoist movement can be traced back to the foundation of Communist Party of Nepal in Calcutta in 1949. The party divided into numerous factions in the 1960s and 1970s. The faction that became the Communist Party of Nepal (Maoist) in 1995, developed in the same year the strategy for a "people's war" designed to encircle the city from the countryside.

The Maoists were able to leverage the common experiences of perceived discrimination, marginalization, and exclusion to gain adherents to their ideology and its promise to bring a new social and political order to Nepal. In 1995, the Maoists began a year-long campaign to build support among the peasantry in the western districts of Rolpa, Rukum and Jajarkot. The primary focus of the campaign was to educate the masses on the goals and tactics of the Maoists. The campaign involved sending teams of Maoist cadres into villages, organising peasants to challenge local authorities, and mobilising villagers for infrastructure improvements such as building roads and bridges.[13] The Maoists' message resonated with local populations that experienced extreme poverty and abuse at the hands of local landlords and government officials. The organizing efforts succeeded in their intended effect of galvanizing local support for the Maoist cause.

As the party recognized ethnicity as a politically significant tool, they also built on the traditional Marxist concept of class as a means of unifying marginalised groups and representing their interests. In October of 1995, Maoists intensified their activities in mid-western districts targeting "class enemies." The government considered this as a "law and order" problem and launched a repressive campaign called "Operation Romeo." This resulted in the

---

12 Mukta Tamang, "Social Movements and Inclusive Peace in Nepal," *Accord* 26, (2017), **https://rc-services-assets.s3.eu-west-1.amazonaws.com/s3fs-public/SocialMovementsAndInclusivePeace.pdf**.

13 See Deepak Thapa, "The Making of the Maoist Insurgency," in *Nepal in Transition: From People's War to Fragile Peace*, eds., Sebastian von Einsiedel, David M. Malone, and Suman Pradhan (New York: Cambridge University Press, 2012) and Li Onesto, *Dispatches from the People's War in Nepal* (London: Pluto Press, 2004).

alienation of a large number of people in the mid-west, which had a long history of deprivation, geographic hardship, lack of development, and strong communist organization in terms of local mobilization. Many critics agree that the counter-insurgent "Operation Romeo" became the trigger for the large number of peoples joining the Maoists' recruit pool. The government's repressive response combined with the latent and widespread grievances experienced by large sectors of the population provided ample potential for further recruitment.

In conclusion, a burgeoning civil society and newly active identity-based parties and movements produced a social awakening in Nepal in the early 1990s. This translated into the use of civil resistance techniques such as *bandhs*. However, strikes and boycotts were largely limited to urban areas. Furthermore, while many of these demonstrations were organized by members of marginalized communities, the organizers generally occupied relatively privileged positions within those groups, and were frequently detached from the rural population. As such, marginalized communities in the countryside felt detached from this activity and were persuaded by Maoist rhetoric that civil resistance was a tool that could only be used by elites in pursuit of "bourgeois" political goals.

Furthermore, there seems to be a void of peacebuilding strategies during this period. This may have been the result of a combination of undue optimism in the wake of the 1990 democratic transition, the aloofness of Nepali political elites as they focused on trying to weaken their rivals in parliamentary competition, and the fact that the field of peacebuilding generally was still in its infancy.

The result was a deadly combination: heightened awareness of inequality and injustice was best channeled and mobilized by the group that saw taking to arms as the only way out.

STAGE 2: Overt Conflict, 1996–2006

Features of the Conflict Phase

On February 4, 1996, the Maoist party submitted a list of 40 demands with an ultimatum to initiate insurgency if they were not met. The political objectives of the Maoists were comprehensive, but their core demands centered on restructuring the state to end the country's "exploitative and semi-feudal" economy, the creation of autonomous ethnic regions, and the promulgation of a new constitution written by popularly elected representatives.[14]

On February 13, 1996, four days before the ultimatum expired, the Maoists started a violent conflict by attacking police posts in six districts of western, mid-western and eastern Nepal. While in its early stages the conflict was largely confined to the mid-western regions, the way the Maoists presented their struggle proved to be highly effective in drawing people to their cause. Their rhetoric skillfully presented their fight as encompassing aggrieved groups and cutting across class and ethnic boundaries. The use of brutal and indiscriminate force by the police alienated substantial sections of the population and exacerbated the conflict by pushing more people into the Maoist fold.

The Maoists raised the issues of longstanding social exclusion, economic marginalization and unequal political representation of women, Dalits, Janajati and Madhesi communities. This helped them to expand their support base quickly. The Maoists also used coercion in recruitment. In some regions, they adopted a policy in which one member of each household was expected to join the Maoist armed force, the People's Liberation Army (PLA).[15]

As the issues of marginalization became a political issue, all of the competing political forces—the parliamentary parties, the monarchy, as well as the Maoists—responded to and exploited ethnic grievances. The Maoists actively recruited disenfranchised Dalits, indigenous nationalities, and women, followed by the Madhesis later on. They adopted a platform of ethnic and regional autonomy in December of 1996 as part of a deliberate strategy to garner support from marginalized groups and created a Madheshi National Liberation Front in 2000.[16] Even though headed by men from privileged groups, the Maoists had high numbers of Dalits, indigenous nationalities and women in their organisation. Among the upper leadership,

---

14 The Maoist ideologue Dr. Baburam Bhattarai submitted a 40-point demand to Prime Minister Sher Bahadur Deuba on February 4, 1996, before launching an armed struggle against the state. All 40 demands can be found here: **http://nepalitimes.com/article/nation/revisiting-maoist-demands,2860**. Also see: Deepak Thapa, *A Kingdom under Siege: Nepal's Maoist Insurgency, 1996–2003* (London: Zed, 2004).

15 Authors' interview with a Maoist leader in Rolpa, May 2018.

16 Balkrishna Mabuhang, *From Peace Settlement to Political Settlement State Restructuring and Inclusive Measures for Marginalised Groups in Nepal*, IPS Paper 10, Berghof Foundation, 2015, 9.

18 out of 23 district chairs were from historically marginalized groups.[17] The radical ideology of the Maoists made these people feel that Maoists were credible and capable of addressing their demands.[18]

The social, economic, and political domination by one particular group at the expense of all others was a recurring theme in the Maoist repertoire. They raised the question of regional disparity to bring about an end to discrimination towards people living in the Tarai region and remote areas while also calling for an end to discrimination against oppressed ethnic groups and Dalits. This was the message used by the Maoists in their attempt to reach out to their main constituencies—the socially excluded. Their strategy paid off very well in terms of finding willing recruits to their cause.

The Maoists used violence judiciously to push the state away from rural areas, eliminate enemies, collect resources and implement their policies. They used violence and its threat selectively to expand their organisations. Besides killings, Maoists deliberately utilized fear to control the population, particularly in rural areas and in some district headquarters.[19] The fear spread through threat and intimidation, real or implied, and was backed up by both the PLA as well as armed Maoist militias. The use of fear tactics, combined with the mobility of those armed forces, enabled the Maoists to control large swathes of rural territory with limited cadres.

Many of the Maoist campaigns also helped them win broader sympathy. Through "people's court," they delivered justice promptly, against all sorts of exploitation and social aberrations (gambling, consumption of alcohol, domestic violence, money lending, etc.). They also used violence against local elites and state agencies in rural areas and in so doing garnered support from poor peasants. These different tactics helped them control much of the countryside, leaving the government to run only the Kathmandu valley and regional headquarters.

Until the end of the 1990s, fighting remained at a relatively low level, and the government's response was restricted to deploying the police rather than the military. Maoists also created various liberation fronts, representing the different "nationalities" of the country, a strategy used to great effect as the Maoists expanded eastward and southward from their stronghold in the mid-western hills.[20] In the initial period, the deaths were overwhelmingly concentrated

---

17 Mukta Lama, "Culture, Caste, and Ethnicity in the Maoist Movement," *Studies in Nepali History and Society* 11, no. 2 (2006): 326.

18 Authors' interview with a Maoist leader in Rolpa, May 2018.

19 Authors' interviews in Dang, Pyuthan and Rolpa, 2018.

20 Maoists formed eleven ethnic and regional based frontier organisations.

in the Maoist strongholds of the mid and far-west regions, but after 2001 fighting and killings spread out across the country, reflecting the military and recruitment success of the Maoists.[21]

International actors, especially European donor governments, began to shift their strategy and focus on a multi-track approach.

Up until 2000, many international actors operating in Nepal had adopted a strategy of avoidance, trying to conduct development and aid programs in a "business as usual" fashion rather than attempt to engage directly in efforts to promote political dialogue. But after 2000, the insurgents began to target internationally funded development programs, threatening the safety and security of local staff. As a consequence, international actors, especially European donor governments, began to shift their strategy and focus on a multi-track approach. On the development front, they refined their aid programs to try to make them more inclusive and sensitive to the social dynamics that were driving the conflict. On the political front, they began meeting with both insurgents and state officials to exert external pressure on them to commence negotiations and reach a settlement to the conflict.[22]

Other foreign governments, however, took a different approach, choosing instead to supply arms and training to government security forces while at the same time calling for a peaceful settlement to the conflict. The king was able to take advantage of the 9/11 terrorist attacks to frame the fight against the Maoists as part of the "Global War on Terror." The United States, India, Britain, Belgium and China all became suppliers of military hardware to the Nepali Army.[23] The result was that the army was transformed from a largely decorative force into a battle-hardened military with modern weaponry. The government ruled out all negotiation with the Maoists and was determined to achieve total victory through force. At the same time, the rebels also stepped up their operations by demolishing bridges, blowing up electricity stations and torturing—and often executing—their opponents.

21　Deepak Thapa, "The Making of the Maoist Insurgency," in *Nepal in Transition: From People's War to Fragile Peace*, eds., Sebastian von Einsiedel, David M. Malone, and Suman Pradhan (New York: Cambridge University Press, 2012), 37-57.

22　Bishnu Sapkota and Bishnu Raj Upreti, "Case Study on Nepal: Observations and Reflections on the Peace and Constitution Making Process," Geneva: SwissPeace, 2017. Available at: **http://swisspeace.ch/fileadmin/user_upload/pdf/Mediation/Nepal_Case_Study_-_National_Dialogue_Handbook.pdf.**

23　India played a particularly quixotic role in the conflict. On the one hand, they were a major supplier of arms to the Nepali Army and even declared the Maoists as terrorists before the Nepal government did so. At the same time, India allegedly provided shelter and safe crossing to Maoist leaders in India during the insurgency period. See S.D. Muni, "Bringing the Maoists Down from the Hills: The Role of India," in *Nepal in Transition: From People's War to Fragile Peace*, eds., Sebastian von Einsiedel, David M. Malone, and Suman Pradhan (New York: Cambridge University Press, 2012), 313-331.

Peacebuilding Strategies

The Maoist campaign from 1996 through the early 2000s shows the bloody consequences of heightened awareness of injustice in the absence of sufficient civil resistance and peacebuilding strategies to channel grievances and frustration into action through nonviolent means. In fact, rather than peacebuilding, the strategy pushed by the dominant international actors (especially after the 9/11 terrorist attacks) was to support the state in an effort to achieve a decisive military victory. This effort effectively stopped Maoist advances, but dramatically escalated the level of bloodshed.

As Maoists took control of almost all of the countryside and the number of fatalities rose, ending conflict through dialogue became a top priority of the government. In 2001, the newly elected prime minister announced a ceasefire which was reciprocated by the Maoists, creating national hope for peace. However, the dialogue and negotiation did not go smoothly since the government negotiators were not able to effectively address the demands of the Maoists[24]. Upon leaving the negotiations, Maoists attacked, for the first time, an army barracks in Dang on November 23, 2001. In reaction to this, the government declared a state of emergency on November 26th and mobilised its army.

This dialogue attempt, although unsuccessful, was strategically important for both the Nepali government and the Maoists. The government was able to create some hope amongst citizens that it could perhaps bring the Maoists into peaceful politics through negotiation. For the Maoists, the dialogue was beneficial on several fronts. First, the Maoists were able to directly discuss their agenda with civil society leaders, who had been invited to participate in the negotiations. This laid the foundation for a relationship between civil society and the Maoists that would later prove important. Second, the Maoists signaled to the international community that they were open to a negotiated settlement to the conflict. This too would pay dividends later in generating pressure on the regime to concede to some Maoist demands. Finally, the cease-fire gave the Maoists an opportunity to re-organize and re-position their combatants.

In October 2002, the king removed the prime minister from his post on the pretext that he had failed to hold parliamentary elections as scheduled. The mainstream parliamentary parties took to the streets to protest against the ousting of the elected prime minister. The government and the Maoists declared a ceasefire on January 29, 2003 to pursue negotiations excluding the parliamentary parties from the process.

---

24 The Maoist demands included a roundtable conference, an interim government and a constituent assembly that would write a republic constitution. The negotiators representing the government were not mandated to discuss a new constitution.

Like in 2001, the main demand of the Maoists was drafting a new constitution through an elected constituent assembly, a request that the government negotiators did not have the authority to approve and which the palace was not interested in granting. Despite this, the negotiations continued. However, the Nepali Army then attacked a Maoist meeting house in Ramechap, killing 17 unarmed Maoist activists and two civilians. This caused the Maoists to pull out from dialogue and the country again lapsed into violence.

By 2003, the conflict had reached both a military as well as a political stalemate. The Maoists continued to control significant territory but were unable to advance further and could see no viable path toward taking total control of the state. Meanwhile, the regime was similarly unable to fully defeat the Maoists. While this created incentives for negotiation, neither side was willing to make sufficient compromises in order to reach a peace deal.

Civil Resistance Strategies

Throughout the early 2000s, both the Maoists and the mainstream political parties increased their use of civil resistance tactics in efforts to strengthen their negotiating positions. The Maoists leveraged their ethnic fronts and student groups to mount street protests and strikes in areas under their control.[25]

Meanwhile, the political parties attempted to utilize protest tactics to confront the king's attempts to consolidate power. However, their mobilization was weak, and while the king temporarily re-instated the prime minister, the parties' inability to muster large mobilization emboldened the monarch. Citing a steady deterioration of conditions in the country in February 2005, the king dismissed the elected government and assumed more direct political control before seizing absolute power. He declared a state of emergency, detained all the major political party leaders and gave the army free rein to engage in more aggressive operations against the Maoists and any other political opposition.

The parties once again turned to civil resistance. This time, they were supported by a coalition of professional organizations and pro-democracy civil society organizations (CSOs) who provided larger numbers of supporters than the traditional political parties could muster on their own. As the analyst Kanak Mani Dixit writes, "In fact, for some time it was the civil society which had to keep the flame of dissent burning, because the parties just couldn't bring in the people."[26]

---

25 Mahendra Lawoti, "Evolution and Growth of the Maoist Insurgency in Nepal," in *The Maoist Insurgency in Nepal: Revolution in the Twenty-First Century*, eds. Mahendra Lawoti and Anup K. Pahari, 3–30, (London: Routledge, 2010), 13.

26 Kanak Mani Dixit, "The Spring of Dissent: People's Movement in Nepal," *India International Center Quarterly* 33, no. 1 (Summer 2006): 114.

The civil society organizations not only boosted the turnout of street protests, they also put pressure on the political parties to put aside their differences and coordinate their strategies of dissent. This led Nepali political parties across the spectrum to form the Seven-Party Alliance (SPA).

Most importantly, however, civil society leaders expressed sympathy for the Maoist causes, if not their methods, and began to float the idea of dialogue with the Maoists, including the possibility of conceding to their primary political demand: elections for a constituent assembly that would draft a new constitution for the country.

The leaders of the SPA were reluctant to consider such dialogue. Simply meeting with the Maoists was perceived as rewarding them for their use of violence, while conceding to a constituent assembly involved jettisoning the constitution that they viewed as the crown jewel of their prior 1990 civil resistance campaign.

Nevertheless, they came to realize that dialogue with the Maoists was necessary in order to develop the breadth of popular support they needed in order to mount a civil resistance campaign that could effectively challenge the king's increasingly autocratic rule. A deal with the Maoists could boost their efforts at mass mobilization in three ways. First, if the Maoists turned out their supporters for the protests, this alone would significantly increase their numbers. Second, a ceasefire with the Maoists would reduce the risks associated with traveling from the countryside to Kathmandu, making it easier for Nepalis from across the country to participate in the major protests in the capital. And finally, by aligning the campaign with the prospect of ending the civil war, rather than just returning their own parties to power, they could encourage politically non-aligned Nepalis to join the movement. As a trade union activist described to Paul Routledge, "...with the Maoists brought in, the hope could be for democracy and peace."[27]

By aligning the campaign with the prospect of ending the civil war ... they could encourage politically non-aligned Nepalis to join the movement.

For the Maoists, a coalition with the political parties offered a way out of the military and political stalemate with the regime. By getting the SPA to agree to their core demand—a constituent assembly—they believed that if the joint campaign were successful, they could use the constitution-writing process to realize their other policy goals.

Maoist and SPA leaders met in New Delhi in the fall of 2005 for a series of negotiations brokered by the Indian government. In November, they signed a document that was known as the "12-point Understanding." The deal essentially consisted of two parts. On the one hand,

---

27 Paul Routledge. "Nineteen Days in April: Urban Protest and Democracy in Nepal," *Urban Studies* 47, no. 6 (2010): 1287.

the political parties agreed to major parts of the Maoist agenda of social justice and state reform to provide redress for structural and historical discrimination against various social, ethnic, caste and other groups. On the other, the Maoists agreed to join the political parties in a united campaign of civil resistance to compel the king to end emergency rule, re-instate political parties, and hold new elections.

Despite the agreement, the two sides continued to act in a largely uncoordinated manner in early 2006, perhaps testing one last time to see if they could achieve their goals without having to rely on the other side for help. Neither side publicly disclosed the signing of the 12-point Understanding, and the Maoists even broke a cease-fire agreement on January 14th, attacking police outposts just outside Kathmandu.

However, both sides quickly realized that continuing on their own would result in defeat. The Maoist military advances stalled while the SPA continued to struggle to generate turnout in their protest efforts. Leaders from each group met again in Delhi in March and signed a new accord committing to work together in a joint campaign that would begin with a general strike on April 6th.[28]

The Maoists, the political parties, and civil society organizations all played crucial roles in launching and sustaining the campaign that became known as the *Jana Andolan II*. The political parties mobilized their cadres and student organizations, while the Maoists reportedly bussed in over 100,000 supporters from the rural districts under their control.[29]

Diverse sections of society and political actors mobilised in daily rallies and demonstrations across the country for 19 days until King Gyanendra restored the parliament he had dissolved in May 2002. Earlier political movements of 1950, 1979 and 1990 were largely ideological, urban-based and elitist in nature. However, this movement covered the entire country. It stimulated the participation of all sections of society transcending the differences of geographical, ideological, social, and economic interests, among others, thus binding citizens together in solidarity and into a common identity. The movement also received the tremendous support and participation of Nepali diasporas, global civil society and the international community. This external pressure helped to propel the movement, and its outcome. International support included withholding arms supplies, curtailing aid, issuing statements on the violation of human rights and extending cooperation to political parties and civil society for fighting for democracy, human rights and peace.

---

28 Aditya Adhikari, *The Bullet and the Ballot Box: The Story of Nepal's Maoist Revolution* (London: Verso, 2014), 192.

29 Ibid.

Impact

Nepal's civil war is remarkable for the fact that it concluded with a transition from a strategy of primarily armed insurgency to one of primarily nonviolent tactics. While the Maoists maintain that the "People's War" had been essential in raising the issues of inequality and discrimination and uniting Nepal's diverse oppressed groups under the banner of a single movement, in only 19 days of civil resistance the Maoists were able to achieve what 10 years of civil war had not.

Key to the success of the campaign was not just the turn to civil resistance strategies, but the combination of civil resistance and peacebuilding approaches. Dialogue and negotiations between the SPA and the Maoists were key to creating both a unified opposition as well as a coalition with sufficiently broad support to engage in effective civil resistance. Moreover, the demonstrated ability of the two sides to work together created additional momentum for the movement as Nepalis began to see the joint movement as the best chance of moving toward a peace agreement. As a trade union activist described to Paul Routledge, "Immediately after the 12-point agreement, the mass meetings of the political parties took on a different flavour, because with the Maoists brought in, the hope could be for democracy and peace."[30]

Conversely, civil resistance served an important pre-negotiation function, clarifying power dynamics between actors, drawing international attention, and helping to build trust that paved the way for dialogue. First, the political parties' civil resistance efforts of 2005 made apparent their need to try to form a coalition with the Maoists. Until 2005, the political parties had been unwilling to consider accommodation of the Maoist platform, often taking a harder line than even the king. But the king's consolidation of power beginning in 2003, combined with the meagre turnout of their efforts to launch demonstrations on their own, changed their calculus, pushing them not only to consider negotiation, but to agree to many of the Maoists' key social and political demands.

Second, while the SPA-led protests were insufficient to truly challenge the king, they revealed the precariousness of his rule to the degree that the Maoists came to view the political parties, rather than the king, as the more viable negotiating partner.

Third, the use of civil resistance strategies drew international support. The international community, especially India, switched from supporting heavy-handed regime repression

---

30 Paul Routledge, "Nineteen Days in April: Urban Protest and Democracy in Nepal," *Urban Studies* 47, no. 6 (2010): 1287.

of the Maoist insurgency to encouraging and even mediating dialogue among the king's political opponents.

Finally, by engaging in a coordinated civil resistance campaign, the Maoists and the SPA were able to build trust that would aid the two sides as they attempted to forge a final peace agreement in the conflict settlement stage.

STAGE 3: Conflict Settlement, 2006–2008

Features of the Conflict Phase

The 19-day movement of April, 2006 led to the restoration of Parliament and opened the door for further negotiating progress between the Seven Party Alliance and the Maoists to bring an end to the civil war. Both sides declared a cease-fire and began to negotiate and implement a series of agreements fleshing out the sequence of steps towards the agreed objective of elections for a Constituent Assembly (CA).

In the aftermath of the movement, both sides formed exclusively male three-member negotiation teams. The SPA and the Maoists had very different visions for Nepal's future and negotiations were driven by each side's interest in securing the political power necessary to implement their ideological agenda. Talks between the two sides were sporadic and lacked formal dialogue mechanisms. Even the designated negotiation "facilitators" were eventually excluded from the process as talks proceeded between group leaders behind closed doors.[31] Though civil society groups played an important role paving the way for the April movement, their involvement afterwards was minimal. Some of the individuals were appointed to the 30- member National Monitoring Committee on Code of Conduct for Ceasefire. International involvement remained low-profile and supportive.

Despite these departures from standard peacebuilding "best practices," negotiators from the both sides continued the peace talks and the negotiations rather quickly bore fruit. On June 16th, Prachanda, the top Maoist leader, made his first public appearance in Kathmandu and signed an eight-point agreement with the SPA.[32] According to the agreement, the internal political boundaries of Nepal would be reformulated, Constituent Assembly elections would be held, and a request would be made for the UN to monitor each sides' armed forces. This agreement remained a crucial basis for the subsequent negotiations. Despite ups and downs, negotiations eventually culminated in a Comprehensive Peace Agreement (CPA) which was signed on November 21, 2006 and declared a lasting end to the armed conflict.

The CPA built upon the principles laid-out in the 12-Point Understanding that had been negotiated a year earlier. This framework committed the Maoists to multi-party democracy, human rights and the rule of law and it committed the SPA to acceptance of the election of a Constituent Assembly to determine Nepal's future form of government. The CPA went further than the 12-Point Understanding on issues of identity and inequality, promising an end

---

31 Authors' interview with Daman Nath Dhungana, who was one of the facilitators of the official peace talks between the government and the Maoists in 2001 and 2003, August 2018.

32 The agreement can be found at: **https://peacemaker.un.org/sites/peacemaker.un.org/files/NP_060616_ Eight%20Point%20Agreement.pdf**.

to policies and institutions that discriminated on the basis on caste, class, religion and gender, including against Dalit, Janajati and Madhesi groups.[33]

Another major issue in the CPA was the integration of the two sides' armed forces. The CPA incorporated the basic arrangements for the cantonment of the combatants of the Maoist army, the restriction of the Nepali Army to its barracks, and the storage of the arms and ammunitions of both sides. 31,152 Maoist personnel were confined in 7 main and 21 satellite sites around the country, and 3,475 weapons were registered.

But in order to make speedy progress toward an agreement, the CPA left several key issues unresolved or open to conflicting interpretations. Questions pertaining to the role of the king, the federal structure of the state, the integration of the armed forces, and the rights of minorities would generate continued conflict in the years that followed. Disputes between the parties, a wave of protests in the Tarai region, and logistical challenges all forced the promised Constituent Assembly elections to be delayed. A subsequent series of negotiations leading to an additional "23-Point Agreement" in December 2007 was needed before the CA elections could eventually be held in April 2008.

Peacebuilding Strategies

The path toward the signing of the CPA was in many ways paved by the efforts at peacebuilding and civil resistance in the latter years of the overt conflict phase. The prior negotiations and agreements reached in Delhi in the fall of 2005 had built some degree of trust between the two sides and provided an overarching framework for what a peace agreement would look like. Meanwhile, the civil resistance campaigns had both a) sobered (somewhat) the mainstream political parties' overly rosy beliefs about their own popularity, thus making them more accommodating to Maoist demands; and b) raised both expectations and momentum that a deal could and should be reached. Support from international actors, as well as an incremental approach through which several smaller deals were signed over the summer of 2006, also appear to have facilitated progress toward a final agreement.

Meetings were hosted by the SPA-led government, and generally had an informal nature, without a formal chair, mediator, or even recorded minutes.[34]

More controversially, as mentioned earlier, the actors participating in negotiations were quite limited, including only 3-member teams of senior (male) leaders from each side. A small

---

33 See: 3.5 of CPA. An unofficial translation of the full text of the CPA is available at: **https://peacemaker.un.org/sites/peacemaker.un.org/files/NP_061122_Comprehensive%20Peace%20Agreement%20between%20the%20Government%20and%20the%20CPN%20%28Maoist%29.pdf**.

34 Farasat, Warisha and Priscilla Hayner, *Negotiating Peace in Nepal: Implications for Justice* (New York: International Center for Transitional Justice, 2009), 15.

handful of civil society leaders were also present at some sessions. Perhaps as a consequence, the final CPA was silent or ambiguous on many of the issues most important to marginalized and excluded communities. Most notably, the CPA did not make any statements concerning whether and to what degree the new political system would have a federal structure. Instead, it made only broad principled statements about transforming the "existing centralized and unitary state system" and creating a more "inclusive, democratic, and progressive" Nepal. How this would look in practice was left to the future Constituent Assembly. Keeping the number of actors at the negotiating table small, handling contentious issues with broad aspirational language, and deferring difficult decisions to the Constituent Assembly were probably all helpful in maintaining momentum toward an agreement and ensuring that civil war did not resume. However, it also raised the potential for conflict in the agreement's aftermath. In fact, unresolved issues came to the fore so quickly that, in our view, the signing of the CPA did not really represent the end of the conflict settlement phase.

In early 2007, the "mainstream" political parties and the Maoists formed an interim government in which Maoists ministers held 5 out of 22 cabinet positions. The goal was for the interim government to move quickly toward national elections for a Constituent Assembly which would draft and implement a new constitution of the country. However, as political disagreements and logistical delays made it clear that elections would not be able to be held by the target date of November 2007, the Maoists became concerned that a loss of momentum would jeopardize their political agenda and potentially even create an opportunity for the king to re-insert himself into politics.

Therefore, in August 2007, the Maoists demanded immediate action on one of their core issues: the official end of the monarchy as a political institution in Nepal. The Maoists called for the declaration of a republic either by vote of the Interim Legislature or by a referendum that would occur before the CA elections. The Nepali Congress party refused, insisting that the future of the monarchy should be decided instead by the first session of the elected CA. The Maoists responded by resigning their posts in the interim government on September 18th, and initiating a series of street protests.

However, despite the resignations and protests, all sides continued with negotiations to resolve the escalating tensions. Finally, on December 23rd, the Maoists and the Seven Party Alliance signed a 23-Point Agreement. The agreement declared that Nepal should be a federal democratic republic but that the republic would be implemented at the first meeting of the CA. In the meantime, the prime minister (as opposed to the king) was to conduct all the duties of the Head of State. With the signing of this agreement, the Maoists re-joined the interim government on December 30th.

Elections for the Constituent Assembly were held on April 10, 2008 in a generally orderly and peaceful atmosphere. In an electoral system that featured a combination of "first-past-the-post" and proportional allocation of seats, the Maoists emerged as the largest party in the CA. Despite reservations, the major political parties accepted the results. The country now had an elected assembly that would attempt to resolve outstanding political disputes through the creation of a new constitution. The Maoist leader, Pushpa Kamal Dahal, most commonly referred to by his nom-de-guerre "Prachanda," became the first prime minister of the "Republic of Nepal."

Civil Resistance Strategies

In the six-month period following the *Jana Andolan II*, during which the CPA was being negotiated, the use of civil resistance strategies was fairly limited. The success of the movement combined with the ongoing negotiations created an environment of relief and hope that dialogue between the parties would yield an end to the civil war. The mobilizations during the *Jana Andolan II* had been spearheaded primarily by three groups: the Seven Party Alliance, the Maoists, and civil society organizations. All three had a greater interest in seeing negotiations proceed than experiencing a return to protest. Moreover, the language of the CPA was sufficiently ambiguous such that all actors could interpret it as being consistent with their values and interests. Indeed, a central pillar of the CPA was that many of the important details were to be addressed in the future by an elected Constituent Assembly.

Many actors, however, did have concerns about the language of the CPA. Advocates for indigenous, Dalit, and marginalized regional groups worried about whether promised protections would ultimately make their way into the constitution. Most contentious was the idea of federalism: many of the organizations advocating on behalf of marginalized communities sought a devolved political structure with highly autonomous federal regions that geographically aligned with the settlement patterns of their respective ethnic and religious groups.

Many members of the Tarai community do not speak Nepali and share ethnic and kinship ties with communities across the border in India.

During the negotiations for the CPA, these groups were willing to press for the agenda through intermediaries—particularly the Maoist negotiators. This changed following the signing of the CPA and the promulgation of the interim constitution. In January 2007, members of Nepal's Madhesi community took to the streets for three weeks of protest. The term "Madhesi" refers to a collective identity of individuals living in the southern plains region of Nepal, known as the Tarai. Many members of this community do not speak Nepali and share ethnic and kinship ties with communities across the border in India. During the latter half of the civil war, the Maoists had proactively sought support from the Madhesis, offering promises of advocating for their goals of political rights and federal autonomy. But by early 2007, Madheshi leaders came to see the Maoists as reneging on their promises, failing to adequately push for federalism in either the CPA or the interim constitution.

The protests were less disciplined than those of the *Jana Andolan II* and were frequently portrayed as "riots" in the media. The state responded with heavy-handed and lethal force against demonstrators. Nevertheless, the movement was in many ways effective in advancing the Madhesis' political agenda. The political parties conceded to the demands for federalism and redistribution of electoral constituencies on the basis of population size as well as ethnically based representation.

The Maoists also began using civil resistance tactics, such as protests and general strikes, to strengthen their bargaining position vis-à-vis the mainstream political parties in the lead-up to the CA elections. Most notably, they took to the streets in August of 2007 to press for an immediate end of the monarchy and declaration of Nepal as a republic. Yet the Maoists' behaviour went beyond the boundary of nonviolent civil resistance tactics when they resorted to sporadic targeted violence. Their cadres, particularly members of the Young Communist League, engaged in threats, intimidation, and beatings. They took individuals into custody and engaged in other quasi-policing activities, raising concerns that the Maoists were failing to fully abandon parallel security mechanisms. The intimidation, violence, extortion and extra-legal activities of the YCL badly eroded public confidence that the Maoists were indeed willing to enter a genuinely democratic process. It also undermined the broader public's view of civil resistance tactics as a legitimate means of redressing political grievances.

Nevertheless, as with the Madhesis, the Maoists' use of civil resistance tactics was effective in achieving key political objectives, as the political parties offered concessions, culminating in the December 2007 agreement. The political parties may have believed that giving in to Maoist demands would expedite the path to elections, in which the Maoists would face a backlash for their actions. As Aditya Adhikari writes, "The conventional wisdom among the parliamentary parties, the media, and diplomatic circles was people had had enough of Maoist coercion and violence during the conflict, and that the revolutionaries had little chance of performing well in the election."[35]

This proved to be a miscalculation. Maoist mobilization in 2007 may have in fact helped prepare them for mobilizing voters in the election, while concessions they earned over the mechanisms and procedures of the election helped them to secure a commanding victory.

---

35 Aditya Adhikari, *The Bullet and the Ballot Box: The Story of Nepal's Maoist Revolution* (London: Verso, 2014), 2010-211.

Impact

The conflict settlement stage in Nepal represented an especially difficult challenge as it was not just the settlement of a civil resistance campaign, but of a decade-long civil war that had killed more than 16,000 people. Nevertheless, a combination of civil resistance and peace-building strategies proved remarkably effective in securing a relatively swift end to the conflict. Dialogue that had begun during the period of early conflict, especially the negotiations leading to the 12-Point Agreement, had provided a framework of mutual understanding for what the contours of a potential final settlement might be. Moreover, it had broken barriers on both sides to the prospect of seeking resolution through dialogue rather than military victory. These efforts were supplemented by both sides participating together in a campaign of civil resistance, thus further building trust and creating a widely shared sense of hope and momentum toward peace.

However, as discussed above, the peace settlement left many of the details, such as how the federal structure would look and work in practice, the processes for integrating Maoist combatants into the security forces, and institutions for transitional justice, open for future debate. Thus, we argue that the signing of the 2006 Comprehensive Peace Agreement did not represent the end of the conflict settlement phase. In fact, less than two months later, a new civil resistance campaign broke out in the Tarai region led by members of the Madhesi group that were angered by the failure of the interim constitution to include provisions for ethnically-based federal autonomy. Additionally, the Maoists increasingly used civil resistance tactics as a tool to advance their agenda in negotiations with the mainstream political parties.

The use of civil resistance strategies in this second half of the conflict settlement phase was instrumentally effective in that it increased the power of marginalized groups who were able to gain substantial political concessions in the interim constitution and in the rules that would govern the elections to the Constituent Assembly. But the repeated use of these tactics combined with escalating levels of violence (within, against, and alongside these mobilizations) started to create some political backlash against the groups using them and against the legitimacy of civil resistance tactics themselves, which increasingly became referred to as "agitations," "riots," or "street insurgency."

The successes of this period should not be overlooked. The conflict settlement phase brought an end to a lengthy, bloody civil war, transformed the Maoists from an armed insurgent group into one committed to institutional and electoral politics, and ultimately secured key provisions for the rights of marginalized communities. Nevertheless, some of the very processes and dynamics that made this period successful set the stage for a particularly difficult post-settlement phase, as the newly elected Constituent Assembly was forced to grapple with thorny political issues not addressed in the settlement process and the use of civil resistance tactics increasingly had the effect of exacerbating social divisions rather than balancing power asymmetries.

STAGE 4: Post-Settlement, 2008–Present

Features of the Conflict Phase

The national CA elections of 2008 were a major milestone in the conflict transformation process, creating an institutional body that would be charged with writing a new constitution for the country. In our analysis, this marks the beginning of the "post-settlement" phase, in which formal political institutions become the primary mechanism for social conflicts. The series of agreements reached during the conflict settlement phase would provide some foundation for the content of the new constitution. For example, the interim constitution promulgated in 2007 (and amended after the Madhesi protests) envisioned three major transformations in the country: "from monarchy to republicanism, from civil conflict to peaceful politics, and from non-inclusive state mechanisms to inclusive democracy."[36] But the details of how these aspirational goals would be achieved still needed to be debated, negotiated, and formalized. By leaving many of the issues of structural violence to be dealt with in the post-settlement phase, they quickly became politicized as they became "political footballs" in inter-party competition for state power. Actors frequently used civil resistance tactics, such as boycotts, strikes, and protests, in an effort to hold politicians to their promises, but such efforts often backfired as protesters were accused of disrupting society and hampering efforts at reconciliation.

On one issue, however, progress was quick. Fulfilling commitments made in the 28-Point Agreement signed in December 2007, the Constituent Assembly voted on its very first day to declare Nepal a republic, and to end the political powers of the monarchy. The king was forced to leave the palace, which was subsequently transformed into a museum. While the vote on the issue of the republic was nearly unanimous, political consensus ended there. Other issues, such as the extent and nature of federalism, the integration of the Maoist and state security forces, and justice for crimes committed during the conflict, would paralyze politics for the next seven years.

The debate on federalism in particular dominated politics and was a main cause for the eventual failure of Nepal's first Constituent Assembly. Many advocates saw federalism as an antidote to the widely acknowledged discrimination and injustice against many of Nepal's historically deprived and marginalised communities. The anti-federalists, on the other hand, feared federalism would lead to the social, economic, and political disintegration of Nepal. Federalism became a

Federalism became a powerful symbol for a wider agenda of inclusion ... it became the single most divisive issue, even leading to bloodshed.

---

36 "Nepal's Constitution Building Process, 2006-2015," International IDEA, 2015.
   https://www.idea.int/publications/catalogue/nepals-constitution-building-process-2006-2015.

powerful symbol for a wider agenda of inclusion, which encompasses other institutional reforms to guarantee ethnically proportional representation and a redefinition of Nepali nationalism to recognise the country's ethnic and cultural diversity. At the same time, it became the single most divisive issue, even leading to bloodshed as some protests devolved into violence and were met with lethal repression from state security forces.

Amidst the disputes over longer-term constitutional issues, short-term political battles over parliamentary coalitions and appointments to government positions occurred. Between 2008 and 2013, Nepal had five different prime ministers. Outside of the CA, numerous political actors used civil resistance tactics as an effort to gain additional political leverage. These tactics became such a regular occurrence, that their utility quickly diminished, and even prompted backlash.

With the Constituent Assembly at a deadlock, it was disbanded and new elections were held in 2013. But the second CA made little more progress than the first, until a devastating earthquake in April 2015. The aftermath of the earthquake galvanized political action, resulting in a constitution finally being passed in September 2015. But many marginalized communities viewed the compromises reached to secure its passage as coming at their expense. Madhesis in particular were outraged by provincial borders that seemingly minimized their political power, as well as citizenship rules that limited automatic citizenship to being granted only to children of Nepali fathers, but not Nepali mothers. A major protest campaign broke out in December 2015, with support from the Indian government. Efforts by protestors to block transit across the Nepal-India border resulted in widespread fuel shortages. But rather than pressure the regime to concede to the Madhesis' demands, the suffering created by the fuel shortages sparked anger from other communities and undermined support for the Madhesis. The campaign ultimately ended when India reversed its position and withdrew its support for the Madhesis.

While Nepal has successfully passed a new constitution and experienced no reversion to full-scale civil war, some historically marginalized communities continue to feel excluded from politics. Major disturbances, such as the 2015 Madhes uprising, have resulted in fatalities, and a Maoist splinter group led by Netra Bikram Chand in the far western and mid-western regions continues to pose a risk of future violence. Political parties did not initially take Chand and his group seriously. But on February 22, 2019, the group detonated a bomb outside the office of the national cellular company, killing one citizen and injuring two others.[37] In response,

---

37 "Chand Party warns of retaliation after government bans its criminal activities," *The Kathmandu Post*, March 14, 2019, **https://kathmandupost.com/national/2019/03/14/chand-party-warns-of-retaliation-after-government-bans-its-criminal-activities**.

the government declared the group a criminal outfit in March and arrested dozens of party members over the next seven months, killing two.[38]

Peacebuilding Strategies

With the election of the Constituent Assembly, the peacebuilding process took an institutionalized form. The elected Constituent Assembly became the vehicle through which political and social disagreements would be resolved. However, several obstacles hindered its ability to do so. The first was simply mathematical: as a constitution required a two-thirds majority to pass, it required considerable consensus across diverse factions (both political parties as well as social groups) in order to make political progress. On the one hand, this ensured that no one group could force through its own political agenda. But it also meant that progress was exceedingly slow, creating frustration and disillusionment among the broader population. Moreover, representatives of marginalized communities felt that the need to forge broad consensus meant finding the "lowest common denominator" among political factions, often meaning that they felt pressured to accept terms that offered fewer explicit protections for marginalized groups. Particularly contentious issues included quotas for minority representation in parliament, the level of political devolution to occur in a federal system, and the alignment of provincial boundaries along patterns of ethnic settlement as opposed to other historical or geographical boundaries.

Furthermore, progress was impeded by competition for power both between and within the political parties. While the Maoists had won a plurality of seats, no single political party had a majority, requiring the formation of coalitions. The parties jockeyed to build the largest coalition possible while trying to undermine those of their rivals, while individual politicians campaigned for positions of power within their party or within the government. During the entire period of the first Constituent Assembly, no government completed a full term.

At times, fragmentation among the political parties even threatened a return to violence. Public security remained a matter of concern throughout much of the country. There were widespread complaints that the Maoists continued to engage in a pattern of low-level intimidation and threats against various sectors, particularly businesses in urban areas, leading to protests from the business community. Meanwhile, there had been serious divisions within the party ever since the Maoists decided to enter the peace process and demand a democratic republic. Hardliners in the party, led by Mohan Baidya, claimed that while a "democratic republic" was a tactical goal, the ultimate aim must remain a "people's federal republic" or "people's democracy."

---

38 Durga Lal KC, "Nearly two dozen Chand party cadres arrested in biggest police raid yet on the outfit," *The Kathmandu Post*, October 17, 2019, **https://kathmandupost.com/province-no-5/2019/10/17/police-arrest-21-communist-party-of-nepal-leaders-and-cadres-in-dang**.

Despite fears from other political parties that the Maoists would attempt to pursue a one-party state, Prachanda took several steps to signal his commitment to multi-party politics. Some, such as concessions over the integration of Maoist fighters into the national army, angered factions within his own party. In April 2012, Mohan Baidya declared the entire process to be "surrender and disarmament." After a protracted internal party struggle, the Maoist party finally split in June, with Baidya walking away with several other senior leaders to form another party. Initially, it was feared that his cadres might return to arms again. In the end, they did not. After boycotting the 2013 elections for the second Constituent Assembly—in which the Maoists lost their plurality—some factions from the Baidya-led party re-joined the main Maoist party. However, divisions within the main party remain, as some party members—especially those representing marginalized communities—see the Maoist leadership as having abandoned their priorities in favor of the comforts and privileges of political power in Kathmandu.

In the aftermath of the April 2015 earthquake, the main political parties (the Maoists along with the two leading parties from the former SPA: the Nepali Congress and the Unified Marxist-Leninists) were able to finally achieve consensus and pass a constitution in September of 2015. The Constitution includes many of the provisions that had been central to the Maoist platform as well as those of marginalized communities, including explicit language protecting the rights of religious, ethnic, and caste minorities, the declaration of Nepal as a secular republic, and the creation of a federal system with seven provinces. However, several indigenous and Madhesi groups vehemently opposed the constitution as they felt the borders of the federal provinces were constructed in such a way as to limit their ability to self-rule. The Constitution has also been criticized for favoring the children of male Nepali citizens over those of women in terms of citizenship status. Finally, apart from the Constitution, progress toward transitional justice remains stalled, with political leaders sharing a mutual interest in delaying and weakening investigations into alleged abuses of power that would embarrass themselves and their fellow party cadres.

Part of what has enabled these developments has been a strategic shift by Maoist leadership to rely less on the support of leaders and organizations representing the interests of marginalized ethnic and regional groups and more on coalition politics with other political parties, particularly the Unified Marxist-Leninists. This cooperation culminated in May 2018 with the merger of the two parties into the Nepal Communist Party (NCP). The prime minister and co-chair of the NCP, K.P. Oli, is viewed as a vocal opponent of much of the agenda of marginalized groups, leaving these groups feeling as if they have a limited voice in national politics. Madhesi parties, various indigenous nationalities, and women's groups continue to demand constitutional amendments. However, the major political parties all object to such amendments. Groups representing marginalized communities have differed in their responses.

For example, one of the major Madhesi political parties has chosen to join the government, seemingly to fight corruption from the inside. The other remains in opposition, but has largely remained silent on constitutional issues.

Civil Resistance Strategies

The use of civil resistance tactics proliferated through the post-settlement phase of conflict. As the Madhesis and Maoists both gained important political concessions through the use of these tactics during the settlement phase, they continued to use popular mobilizations as a tool to gain political leverage when they lacked the votes needed to implement their agendas in the Constituent Assembly. Other communities, including indigenous ethnicities, Dalits, and (to a lesser degree) victims of conflict violence, similarly turned to civil resistance tactics to press their claims. More recently, professional groups have employed fasts, strikes, and protests to demand reforms to stop governmental corruption and nepotism within the regulation of their professions. Dr. Govind KC, an orthopaedic surgeon, has been using nonviolence as a means of bringing the attention of concerned authorities to his demands. So far, he has gone on hunger strikes 16 times over the past six years demanding reforms in medical education and services. His campaign has been supported by people of different walks of life including doctors, civil society organisations, editors of leading media houses and the common public. "Solidarity for Dr. KC" and "Save Dr. KC" have become popular slogans to express solidarity with the movement and draw the attention of policymakers. For example, members of the Nepal Medical Association began a hunger strike to push for legislative action to end nepotism, cronyism, and other forms of corruption in the country's medical education system.[39] And women's groups have taken to the streets on multiple occasions to demand justice for victims of sexual violence.[40]

The use of these tactics has been somewhat successful. The government has tried to address concerns about minority inclusion through quotas in education, public employment and political representation. In the civil service, 45 percent of the seats are allocated to marginalized or under-represented groups.

---

39 "Doctors begin mass hunger strike to press government to address Dr. KC's demands," *The Kathmandu Post*, January 29, 2019, **https://kathmandupost.com/national/2019/01/28/doctors-begin-mass-hunger-strike-to-press-government-to-address-dr-kcs-demands**.

40 For a selection of such cases, see: "Nepalese protest violence against women," *Al Jazeera*, January 7, 2013, **https://www.aljazeera.com/news/asia/2013/01/20131714247955976.html**; and "Women march on Kathmandu streets to protest rising rape incidents," *Xinhua*, March 8, 2018, **http://www.xinhuanet.com/english/2018-03/08/c_137025294.htm**.

But the frequent use of civil resistance tactics started to achieve only diminishing returns, and in several cases backfired. At a normative level, critics of the use of civil resistance tactics argued that those with grievances ought to use institutionalized political channels, and that it was fundamentally undemocratic to turn to mass mobilization to try to achieve political goals when a majority support in elected bodies for such goals was lacking. Others countered that what was at stake, especially for marginalized communities, were fundamental rights that are necessary exactly because they would be trampled by majority-rule.

Furthermore, the tactics themselves began to impose a toll on Nepali society. As the most popular tactic, *bandhs,* became increasingly frequent, citizens began to resent being forced to forego work and consequently income. Nepalis feared that violating a *bandh* could result in targeted punishment, including violence, by the protesting groups. Citizens turned to news reports and even online "*bandh* trackers" to keep track of when *bandhs* were threatened or scheduled so that they could plan their lives accordingly.

Yet another reason for civil resistance tactics' loss of legitimacy, and consequently their diminished effectiveness, was domestic backlash against international involvement, both real and perceived. In the aftermath of the civil war, both foreign development agencies and international NGOs made large investments in peacebuilding programs in Nepal. As intergroup inequalities were seen as one of the root drivers of the violent conflict, these programs often supported marginalized communities, including providing substantial grants to local advocacy organizations. In some cases, these advocacy organizations were the ones utilizing civil resistance tactics, creating an opportunity for critics to portray the mobilizations as driven by foreign agendas and interference. For example, a major set of protests spearheaded by the Nepal Federation of Indigenous Nationalities (NEFIN) in 2010 was derided in the media as the "EU bandh" due to significant grants the organization had been awarded by the British Department for International Development (DFID) and other European aid agencies. A consequence was not only failure of the mobilization to achieve its goals, but a subsequent decline in financial support to NEFIN and similar organizations as aid agencies feared damage to their reputation.[41] The government eventually passed new restrictions on foreign contributions to Nepali civil society organizations.

The most dramatic example of popular demonstrations backfiring came in late 2015, surrounding the passage of the new Constitution. Madhesi parties and activists, angered by provisions in the new constitution that they viewed as denying them sufficient regional autonomy,

---

41 Interviews with aid agency employers conducted by the authors indicate that the aftermath of the global financial crisis also played a major role in the decline of international aid. However, foreign agencies not only decreased their total expenditures, they shifted their funding away from directly supporting advocacy organizations and toward programmatic efforts viewed as less controversial. For example, programs focusing on gender discrimination were perceived as less risky than those focusing on ethnic reconciliation.

took to the streets in protest. The results were even bloodier than the 2007 movement. Violent escalations by protesters, met with lethal repression by the regime, resulted in at least 40 deaths. Furthermore, the protesters were aided by the Indian government, who is widely believed to have helped enforce a blockade that severely limited fuel shipments to the entire country. The resulting shortage of fuel prompted a national economic and humanitarian crisis that only hardened inter-group antagonisms. At the same time, the heavy external involvement by India undermined the perceived legitimacy of the movement. Rather than concede to the demands of protesters, Prime Minister K.P. Oli seized the opportunity to rally nationalist sentiment. An amendment to the Constitution offering partial concessions around parliamentary representation provided India a pretext to back down and end its support of the blockade. While Madhesi leaders were adamant that the amendment did not satisfy their demands, the withdrawal of Indian support forced them to end their campaign in February 2016.

Impact

After seven years and two different Constituent Assemblies, Nepal's new constitution was adopted on September 20, 2015, written by an elected body and passed with close to a 90 percent majority. This constitution was the culmination of the political transition that began at the end of the armed conflict between the CPN-M and the state. The constitution includes many of the most important demands made by marginalized communities, representing significant progress toward political, economic, and social inclusion since the outbreak of overt conflict in the 1990s. However, it is important to note that the constitution and the process leading to its adoption has in many ways deepened ethnic, social and political fractures that it was supposed to have helped heal.

Since the end of overt conflict, Nepal has seen numerous efforts at peacebuilding through formal institutional channels, international missions, and programs to promote social dialogue. It has also seen the use, and some would argue overuse, of civil resistance tactics in an effort to gain power and leverage over the constitution-writing process. In some ways this has been successful, in that Nepal has not experienced a reversion to large-scale violence. On the other hand, many Nepalis have been unsatisfied with the trajectory of political progress in their country since 2006. Both the continued pervasiveness of structural inequalities as well as continued instability and episodes of violence make Nepal appear far from the desired outcome of sustainable peace and justice.

One particularly troubling question raised by this period is why, despite its robust history in Nepal, has the use of civil resistance appeared to have diminished in its effectiveness and occasionally even backfired in the post-settlement period? Several dynamics could be at play. First, the perceived legitimacy of civil resistance may be different in democratic contexts when institutional methods exist as an alternative. In such cases, tactics of mass mobilization and disruption may be seen by the majority as attempts to subvert democratic processes, while the mobilized minority views them as a necessary tool to prevent majority domination. Second, the frequency of civil resistance tactics appears to have been an issue in Nepal. *Bandhs* became so frequent that they imposed an increasingly high cost on all members of Nepali society as citizens were forced to forego work and pay. Relatedly, the call for general strikes may have been too aggressive as a tactical choice. It may have been too disruptive in society, sparking more resentment than sympathy. A lack of nonviolent discipline was likely another factor, as violent acts committed alongside largely peaceful demonstrations turned off potential sympathizers. Support from external actors turned out to be a liability, allowing opponents to portray marginalized communities resorting to civil resistance as "fifth columns" subservient to foreign interests. Finally, it may be that the use of civil resistance strategies across social cleavages presents unique difficulties when compared to campaigns launched by broad coalitions that include privileged majority groups. It is evident that marginalized groups struggle more to win the support of individuals from other groups, while adversaries have an easier time portraying marginalized groups' demands as illegitimate, their methods as disproportionate, and the use of repression against them as justified.

Key Takeaways

Nepal is in many ways a success story of both civil resistance and conflict transformation. The leaders of a violent insurgency put down their guns in favor of civil resistance and eventually democratic politics. Nepal has not seen a reversion to large-scale violence and successfully passed a democratic constitution in 2015. However, many of the social tensions that initiated the conflict remain unresolved. The outcomes of the post-conflict period produced unfavourable results in the eyes of many historically marginalized communities, especially on issues such as security sector integration, the geography of federal districts, and transitional justice. Consequently, protests are still a regular occurrence and there has even been a proliferation of armed groups in Nepal's southern plains and western hills. Encouragingly, a 2017 survey reported that 94 percent of Nepalis feel safe in their communities.[42] However, this may change after the wave of deadly attacks by Netra Bikram Chand's armed political faction in 2019.

The framework of integrated civil resistance and peacebuilding strategies can help us better understand the ways in which the conflict transformation process has been successful and why in other respects it has fallen short. The case of Nepal reinforces the following lessons that emerge from the framework:

- **Civil resistance and peacebuilding strategies can produce a societal awakening to social injustices, among both oppressed and privileged populations.** The period of democratization in the early 1990s produced new discourses, new civil society organizations, and new social mobilizations around issues of structural inequalities and identity-based oppression.

- **The absence of civil resistance and peacebuilding strategies can result in social frustrations being channeled toward violent alternatives.** As awareness of injustice grew among marginalized groups in Nepal, a lack of peacebuilding strategies and a perception that civil resistance was only used by urban elites for political advantage led rural Nepalis to gravitate toward the Maoists and their program of protracted "People's War."

- **The combination of peacebuilding and civil resistance strategies can be effective in toppling entrenched power structures.** In the end, 19 days of civil resistance accomplished what 10 years of civil war could not, forcing the king to relinquish power.

---

42 The Asia Foundation, *A Survey of the Nepali People in 2017*, Kathmandu: The Asia Foundation, 2018, https://asiafoundation.org/wp-content/uploads/2018/04/Survey-of-the-Nepali-People-in-2017_revised-752018.pdf.

Dialogue and negotiation produced the coalition between the Maoists and political parties that made effective civil resistance possible.

- **The combination of civil resistance and peacebuilding can pave the way for durable conflict settlements.** A mutually understood framework and increased trust forged through dialogue and, later, joint participation in civil resistance allowed the Maoists and the political parties to reach a Comprehensive Peace Agreement only months after the end of the civil resistance campaign.

- **Civil resistance can channel frustrations in the post-settlement stage.** Actors dissatisfied with political developments after the CPA have repeatedly turned to civil resistance tactics to express discontent and seek leverage over those in official positions of power. While there has been fear of escalation to violence, and several violent episodes, there has been no return to large-scale civil war, as has frequently occurred in other post-conflict environments.

However, there are other aspects in which the Nepal case complicates the idealized framework:

- **Marginalized groups may be among the least likely to see civil resistance and peacebuilding strategies as viable solutions to their problems.** There was no lack of awareness of civil resistance as a strategy in Nepal in the early 1990s; a major civil resistance movement had brought democracy to the country in 1990. Nevertheless, civil resistance was widely perceived, especially among oppressed groups, as a strategy of the elite. It was seen as being used by middle-class urbanites in pursuit of political power and as largely irrelevant to the plight of rural, marginalized communities seeking broader social and economic change. While the success of the second *Jana Andolan* in 2006 encouraged indigenous and Madhesi activists to attempt nonviolent action again in the post-conflict period when their political demands were not met, the failure of these efforts may have once again fostered pessimism about the viability of civil resistance for excluded communities. The occasional use of violence by some of these groups, while limited, may be a consequence of that pessimism.[43]

---

43 This dynamic is consistent with one of the co-author's previous works demonstrating that civil resistance is used less frequently by excluded ethnic minorities. See Ches Thurber, "Ethnic Barriers to Civil Resistance," *Journal of Global Security Studies* 3, no. 3 (2018): 255-270.

- **Civil resistance may only partially balance power inequalities, undermining conflict settlements.** The success of civil resistance in Nepal was the result of partnership between marginalized and privileged groups. Because of this, elites were still in a position to dominate post-conflict politics. Perhaps if marginalized groups had continued mobilization through the conflict settlement phase, they might have been able to secure additional protections in the CPA. One reason conflict settlement came so quickly is that it was ambiguous about many of the divisive social issues that had been the original drivers of the conflict. But this is a double-edged sword; attempts at resolving all of these contentious issues in the conflict settlement phase may have risked a return to overt conflict. Furthermore, continuing mobilization during the peace talks might have been perceived as subversive and disruptive, potentially undermining the agendas of those groups advocating for minority rights.

- **Civil resistance sometimes backfires.** Marginalized communities used civil resistance strategies throughout the post conflict stage in an effort to gain leverage over political actors in the way Dudouet's framework suggests. But rather than secure greater justice, these efforts largely seem to have backfired as the broader public perceived these protestors to be causing economic suffering, disrupting social harmony, and risking a return to large-scale violence. Future research might do well to focus on strategies that marginalized and underprivileged groups can employ under such polarizing conditions. Such strategies might include framing grievances to highlight common ideals, forging coalitions that cross traditional social divides, and selecting tactics that reduce the risk of violent escalation. This is another area where drawing on both civil resistance and peacebuilding traditions could be fruitful: civil resistance has focused on reducing social distance and leveraging opponents' dependencies, while peacebuilding has emphasized dialogue in polarized settings.

Cited Bibliography

Adhikari, Aditya. *The Bullet and the Ballot Box: The Story of Nepal's Maoist Revolution*. London: Verso, 2014.

Bhattachan, Krishna. "Ethnopolitics and Ethnodevelopment: An Emerging Paradigm in Nepal—With a Postscript." In *Nationalism and Ethnic Conflict in Nepal: Identities and Mobilization after 1990*, edited by Susan Hangen and Mahendra Lawoti, 35–57. New York: Routledge, 2013.

Bista, Dor Bahadur. *Fatalism and Development: Nepal's Struggle for Modernisation*. New Delhi: Sangam Books, 1991.

Bogati, Subindra. "Assessing Inclusivity in the Post-War Army Integration Process of Nepal." *Inclusive Political Settlements Paper 11*. Berlin: Berghof Foundation, 2015. **https://berghof-foundation.org/library/assessing-inclusivity-in-the-post-war-army-integration-process-in-nepal.**

Bogati, Subindra, Carapic Jovana and Muggah Robert. "The Missing Middle: Examining the Armed Group Phenomenon in Nepal." Geneva, Small Arms Survey, 2013. **https://berghof-foundation.org/library/assessing-inclusivity-in-the-post-war-army-integration-process-in-nepal.**

Brown, T. Louise. *The Challenge to Democracy in Nepal: A Political History*, 177. London: Routledge, 1996.

"Chand Party warns of retaliation after government bans its criminal activities." *The Kathmandu Post*, March 14, 2019. **https://kathmandupost.com/national/2019/03/14/chand-party-warns-of-retaliation-after-government-bans-its-criminal-activities.**

"Comprehensive Peace Agreement between the Government of Nepal and the Communist Party of Nepal (Maoist)." United Nations, 2006. **https://peacemaker.un.org/nepal-comprehensiveagreement2006.**

Curle, Adam. *Making Peace*. London: Tavistock, 1971.

Dixit, Kanak Mani. "The Spring of Dissent: People's Movement in Nepal." *India International Center Quarterly* 33, no. 1 (2006): 113-25.

Dudouet, Véronique. *Powering to Peace: Integrated Civil Resistance and Peacebuilding Strategies*. Washington, DC: International Center on Nonviolent Conflict, 2017.

Farasat, Warisha and Priscilla Hayner. *Negotiating Peace in Nepal: Implications for Justice*. New York: International Center for Transitional Justice, 2009.

Francis, Diana. *People, Peace and Power: Conflict Transformation in Action*. London: Pluto Press, 2002. Francis, Diana. *From Pacification to Peacebuilding*. London: Pluto Press, 2010.

Galtung, Johan. "Violence, Peace, and Peace Research." *Journal of Peace Research* 6, no. 3 (1969): 167-191.

Galtung, Johan. *Peace by Peaceful Means: Peace and Conflict, Development and Civilisation*. London: Sage Publications, 1996.

Hachhethu, Krishna. "The Question of Inclusion and Exclusion in Nepal: Interface Between State and Society." Conference on "The Agenda of Transformation: Inclusion in Nepali Democracy," Social Science Baha, April 24-26, 2003.

KC, Durga Lal. "Nearly two dozen Chand party cadres arrested in biggest police raid yet on the outfit." *The Kathmandu Post,* October 17, 2019. **https://kathmandupost.com/province-no-5/2019/10/17/police-arrest-21-communist-party-of-nepal-leaders-and-cadres-in-dang.**

Lama, Mukta. "Culture, Caste, and Ethnicity in the Maoist Movement." *Studies in Nepali History and Society* 11, no. 2 (2006): 302–54.

Lawoti, Mahendra. "Evolution and Growth of the Maoist Insurgency in Nepal." In *The Maoist Insurgency in Nepal: Revolution in the Twenty-First Century*, edited by Mahendra Lawoti and Anup K. Pahari, 3–30. London: Routledge, 2010.

Lederach, John Paul. *Preparing For Peace: Conflict Transformation Across Cultures*. New York: Syracuse University Press, 1995.

Lederach, John Paul. *Building Peace: Sustainable Reconciliation in Divided Societies*. Washington, DC: United States Institute of Peace (USIP), 1997.

Mabuhang, Balkrishna. "From Peace Settlement to Political Settlement State Restructuring and Inclusive Measures for Marginalised Groups in Nepal." *Inclusive Political Settlements Paper 11*. Berlin: Berghof Foundation, 2015.

Muni, S. D. "Bringing the Maoists down from the Hills: India's Role." In *Nepal in Transition: From People's War to Fragile Peace*, edited by Sebastian von Einsiedel, David Malone, and Suman Pradhan. New York: Cambridge University Press, 2012.

Murshed, S. M. and Scott Gates. "Spatial–Horizontal Inequality and the Maoist Insurgency in Nepal." *Review of Development Economics* 9, no. 1 (2005): 121–34.

"Nepal raises conflict death toll." *BBC News,* September 22, 2009. **http://news.bbc.co.uk/2/hi/8268651.stm**.

"Nepal's Constitution Building Process, 2006-2015." *International IDEA*, 2015. **https://www.idea.int/publications/catalogue/nepals-constitution-building-process-2006-2015**.

Onesto, Li. *Dispatches from the People's War in Nepal*. London: Pluto Press, 2004.

Rai, Om Astha. "What was it all for?" *Nepali Times,* February 5, 2016. **https://archive.nepalitimes.com/article/nation/revisiting-maoist-demands,2860**.

Routledge, Paul. "Nineteen Days in April: Urban Protest and Democracy in Nepal." *Urban Studies* 47, no. 6 (2010): 1279-1299.

Sapkota, B and Bishnu Upreti. "Case Study on Nepal: Observations and Reflections on the Peace and Constitution Making Process." Geneva: SwissPeace, 2017. **http://swisspeace.ch/fileadmin/user_upload/pdf/Mediation/Nepal_Case_Study_-_National_Dialogue_Handbook.pdf**.

Tamang, Mukta S. "Social Movements and Inclusive Peace in Nepal." *Accord* 26, (2017). **https://www.c-r.org/accord/nepal/social-movements-and-inclusive-peace-nepal**.

Thapa, Deepak. *A Kingdom under Siege: Nepal's Maoist Insurgency, 1996-2003*. London: Zed Books, 2004.

Thapa, Deepak. "The Making of the Maoist Insurgency." In *Nepal in Transition: From People's War to Fragile Peace*, edited by Sebastian von Einsiedel, David Malone, and Suman Pradhan, 37–57. New York: Cambridge University Press, 2012.

The Asia Foundation. *A Survey of the Nepali People in 2017*. Kathmandu: The Asia Foundation, 2018. **https://asiafoundation.org/wp-content/uploads/2018/04/Survey-of-the-Nepali-People-in-2017_revised-752018.pdf**.

Thurber, Ches. "Ethnic Barriers to Civil Resistance." *Journal of Global Security Studies* 3, no. 3 (2018): 255-270.

About the Authors

Subindra Bogati is the Founder and Chief Executive of Nepal Peacebuilding Initiative—an organization devoted to evidence-based policy and action on peacebuilding and humanitarian issues. He has been working for conflict transformation and peace process in Nepal through various national and international organizations for the last several years. Currently, he is implementing projects to strengthen capacities for conflict prevention, local mediation and reconciliation at the sub-national levels in Nepal. He holds an M.A. in International Relations from London Metropolitan University and was awarded the FCO Chevening Fellowship in 2009 at the University of Birmingham's Centre for Studies in Security and Diplomacy. He is a Ph.D. candidate in the department of Political Science, Tribhuvan University, Nepal.

Ches Thurber is an Assistant Professor in the Department of Political Science at Northern Illinois University. His research and teaching focus on international security, conflict, and contentious politics. Dr. Thurber has held fellowships at the University of Chicago and Harvard Kennedy School's Belfer Center for Science and International Affairs. He received his Ph.D. and MALD from The Fletcher School of Law and Diplomacy at Tufts University and his B.A. from Middlebury College. His book project, *Between Gandhi and Mao: The Social Roots of Civil Resistance*, investigates how social structures inform movements' willingness to engage in nonviolent and violent strategies. Dr. Thurber's research has been published or is forthcoming in the *International Studies Quarterly, Journal of Global Security Studies,* and *Conflict Management and Peace Science*, among others.